Merry Christmas

_____

From

_____

Date

_____

The Christmas Story

Experiencing
the Most
Wonderful Story
Ever Told

Story

G. A. Myers

HOWARD
PUBLISHING CO.

$\mathcal{O}$ur purpose at Howard Publishing is to:

- *Increase faith* in the hearts of growing Christians
- *Inspire holiness* in the lives of believers
- *Instill hope* in the hearts of struggling people everywhere

Because He's coming again!

03 04 05 06 07 08 09 10 11 12   10 9 8 7 6 5 4 3 2

Edited by Between the Lines
Interior design by Stephanie D. Walker

Library of Congress Cataloging-in-Publication Data
Myers, G. A., 1955–
    The Christmas story / [Gary Myers]
        p. cm.
    ISBN: 1-58229-330-9
    1. Jesus Christ—Nativity—Juvenile literature. I. Title.

BT315.3.M94 2003
232.92—dc22

                                                    2003056606

The stories in this book were previously published under the title *Hugs from Heaven: The Christmas Story*.

Contents

God grant you
the light in Christmas,
which is faith;
the warmth of Christmas,
which is love;
the radiance of Christmas,
which is purity;
the righteousness of Christmas,
which is justice;
the belief in Christmas,
which is truth;
the all of Christmas,
which is Christ.

—Wilda English

The Christmas Story

Introduction

Each year we all look forward to the holidays with anticipation, envisioning a wonderful, storybook Christmas. But sometimes, as the rush of the holiday sets in, it's easy to forget that what makes Christmas so wonderful isn't the presents, the parties, or the decorations. It's the Story—God's love expressed through the birth of His Son Jesus Christ in a manger two thousand years ago. This little book was designed to remind you of the reason you rejoice—to bring you back to the Story of God's intense love for you.

The Christmas Story is arranged in chapters that include a fictional story based on a particular passage in the Christmas story, a poem celebrating Christmas, a Christmas reflection, and a poignant quote.

As you revisit the angelic announcement to Mary, enter the dream of Joseph, and envision the field where the shepherds received news of Christ's coming, my hope is that you will be transported to that manger where all of history was rewritten by the birth of one solitary life.

1

The Announcement to Mary

Little did she know that as the heavens listened, a still, small voice answered: "And I trust you, My child."

ARY TOOK HER POSITION on the roof of the house and began the nightly ritual of brushing through her long, onyx hair. As the sun's orange blaze melted into the soft shades of dusk, Mary raised her nose and sniffed the evening air. She loved this time of year, when the surrounding hills of Nazareth were filled with flowers. Every evening their sweet fragrances would ride the gentle wind into town and chase away the stale odors of animals and swirling dust. The youthful Mary took her perch here each day at the same time, after the evening meal was ended and everything was dutifully put away. She watched the neighborhood children play, and she laughed at their antics. She noticed other things as well.

She watched the men who gathered on the street to talk politics and business and to argue about Scripture. She knew their routine: They would begin their conversation calmly, but after a few minutes, an argument would ensue. It always began with Perez, a long-bearded, elderly man who lived a few houses away. In a hopeless sort of whine, he would complain about how the government was ruining Israel. Several others would join in with a hearty "Amen!" Then Joseph, her Joseph, the man she would soon wed—the man with bright, bold eyes; strong, energetic hands; and a deep, commanding voice—would always stand up on the side of faith and in defense of the promises of God.

That was what she had first loved about her Joseph: his faith—his strong, confident faith. Faith was in short supply in Israel at present, and she loved listening to Joseph proclaim to the group that the Messiah was coming, and coming very soon. The others would mumble under their breath about the hundreds of years since God had spoken in Israel. Did God still care about His people? Did He hear their cries? Joseph regularly concluded his discourse with, "Go ahead and hide behind your doubt if you wish; the God of my forefathers is faithful, and He will do what He has promised."

> Mary suddenly felt a strong desire to be secluded, so alone that she would feel only the closeness of the God she loved and believed in.

His words blew over Mary like a strong, refreshing wind. She whirled around and fell to her knees. With her arms uplifted, her long hair catching the south wind, she prayed, "God, thank you for hearing me; thank you for blessing my life with the words of the man with whom I will soon be one. I do believe You hear me when I pray. Send Messiah to us, O God. Send Him on the faithful prayers of Your servants who have not surrendered their faith. We wait for our deliverer, strong and mighty." With her eyes moist with tears of joy and hope, Mary rose and lifted her head to the now visible stars. She spoke her last five words forcefully and repeated them three times: "We trust you, O God." Little did she know that as the heavens listened, a still, small voice answered: "And I trust you, My child."

Mary suddenly felt a strong desire to be secluded, so alone that she would feel only the closeness of the God she loved and believed in. She moved from the roof to her small room, fell to her knees once more, and raised her voice in joyous praise. Although she thought she was alone, she was not. Although she believed her prayers were being heard only by God, they were not. When Mary opened her eyes, she saw a bright glow emanating from behind her. She stood, turned, and stepped back in shock as the angelic being before her appeared in what seemed the radiance of a million candles.

"Greetings, you who are highly favored! The Lord is with you," Gabriel said. "Do not be afraid, Mary; you have found favor with God." The young woman began to feel the warmth of an invisible embrace. Assurance quickly replaced her fear as she listened intently. "You will be with child and give birth to a son, and you are to give Him the name Jesus. He will be great and will be called the Son of the Most High. The Lord God will give Him the throne of His father David, and He will reign over the house of Jacob forever; His kingdom will never end."

As the news settled into Mary's heart, her expression changed from astonishment to bewilderment, and she asked, "How will this be, since I am a virgin?"

Gabriel moved closer and reached out to touch her shoulder softly. As he felt her nervousness subside, he smiled and said, "The Holy Spirit will come upon you, and the power of the Most High will overshadow you. So the holy one to be born will be called the Son of God."

> She looked deeply into Gabriel's kind eyes and said, "I am the Lord's servant. May it be to me as you have said."

Mary felt the astonished, unutterable question rising within her: *The Messiah...are you talking about Messiah— coming through me?*

Sensing her doubt, Gabriel affirmed, "Even Elizabeth your relative is going to have a child in her old age, and she who was said to be barren is in her sixth month. For nothing is impossible with God."

As Mary lifted her head, the words echoed in her heart until she fully believed them. She looked deeply into Gabriel's kind eyes and said, "I am the Lord's servant. May it be to me as you have said."

After Gabriel left her, Mary stood in silence for a

few moments and then made her way once more to the roof and gazed up to heaven. Exhausted, excited, and exuberant all at the same time, she collapsed to her knees, her arms too weak to raise, and once more emphasized the words through a whisper: "I trust You, O God."

Somewhere in the silence she thought she heard a whisper return on the wind: "And I trust you, My child."

The *Announcement* to Mary

Luke 1:26–38

In the sixth month, God sent the angel Gabriel to Nazareth, a town in Galilee, to a virgin pledged to be married to a man named Joseph, a descendant of David. The virgin's name was Mary. The angel went to her and said, "Greetings, you who are highly favored! The Lord is with you."

Mary was greatly troubled at his words and wondered what kind of greeting this might be. But the angel said to her, "Do not be afraid, Mary, you have found favor with God. You will be with child and give birth to a son, and you are to give him the name Jesus. He will be great and will be called the Son of the Most High. The Lord God will give him the throne of his father David, and he will reign over the house of Jacob forever; his kingdom will never end."

"How will this be," Mary asked the angel, "since I am a virgin?"

The angel answered, "The Holy Spirit will come upon you, and the power of the Most High will overshadow you. So the holy one to be born will be called the Son of God. Even Elizabeth your relative is going to have a child in her old age, and she who was said to be barren is in her sixth month. For nothing is impossible with God."

"I am the Lord's servant," Mary answered. "May it be to me as you have said." Then the angel left her.

The Mother of God

The threefold terror of love;
   a fallen flare
Through the hollow of an ear;
Wings beating about the room;
The terror of all terrors that I bore
The Heavens in my womb.

Had I not found content
   among the shows
Every common woman knows,
Chimney corner, garden walk,
Or rocky cistern where we tread
   the clothes
And gather all the talk?

What is this flesh I purchased with
   my pains,
This fallen star my milk sustains,
This love that makes my heart's
   blood stop
Or strikes a sudden chill
   into my bones
And bids my hair stand up?

           —*William Butler Yeats*

Christmas Reflections

It may have happened two thousand years ago, but within its story lines lives the most encouraging and inspiring message of all time. If you allow the hustle of holiday shopping to push you past Christmas and into the new year panting and breathless, you will most certainly miss it. But don't. The message of the Story has little to do with presents and packages, and everything to do with you. It can be summed up in one simple, but wonderfully, true statement: God entrusts extraordinary things to very ordinary people.

You see this truth right there in the lives of the participants in this blessed event—Mary the poor virgin, Joseph the blue-collar carpenter, and shepherds baby-sitting smelly sheep in a field.

If you were to describe the Christmas story as a portrait, you would have to say that the characters in the story were like rough, frayed burlap on which the golden brush of God painted the most precious moment in history. If you and I had painted the portrait, however, we would certainly have painted it on the finest canvas, and our characters would have been more worthy types—kings, wealthy aristocrats, responsible citizens, esteemed leaders. But we didn't paint it; God did.

And if you look into the beauty of God's portrait, you will plainly see a reflection. That's right, a reflection of your face, your weaknesses, your struggles, your future, and your ordinariness. Why? Because that's the kind of person to whom God entrusts His precious plans and purposes.

Do you feel you're just an ordinary person with an average life in a commonplace world? Good. You're just what God is looking for. You may be called upon to care for a special child, soothe a hurting soul, or bring light to a lonely life. Just don't let the glory of the Story pass you by. Stop, look, and listen. He trusts you to fulfill His mission.

Someday someone may describe you as a burlap background on which God used His golden brush to paint a precious moment in history. In fact, the painting may already be under way.

God is

of human his

AND HE

continuous

God is the God of human history, AND HE IS AT WORK continuously, *mysteriously,* accomplishing HIS ETERNAL PURPOSES IN US, *through us, for us,* AND IN SPITE OF US.

—Elisabeth Elliot

2

Joseph's Dilemma

He could easily put up
with the off-color remarks
and snickers, but what
about her? It would destroy
this beautifully spiritual
woman he had learned
to love so deeply.

 OSEPH'S MOOD MIRRORED the darkening sky as he trudged down the familiar, dusty streets of Nazareth toward his carpentry shop. A clutter of noises filled the air: shopkeepers closing their stores; scampering feet responding to the harmonizing calls of moms from a hundred doorways; and the last bit of laughter, gossip, and good-nights, which signaled the end of a busy day in the small town. Joseph usually stopped to listen to this symphony of sound, but tonight he heard nothing but his own confused thoughts.

Under normal circumstances he would be heading home to wash off the sawdust and wood shavings that had accumulated in his beard and clothes throughout the day. But he knew he would not be going home this evening or even later tonight. The news he had just received from the woman he was soon to marry left him feeling haunted, hurt, and helpless; and there was only one place he could go to think.

Some men get drunk after receiving such news, others try to act as though they never received it at all, and still others immerse themselves in their work. Joseph was one of those who did the latter. As he pulled open the door of his shop and heard the familiar creak of the hinges, he suddenly relived the shock of hearing Mary say the words, "I'm going to have a baby."

Chapter 2

Her insistence that she had not been with another man rang in his ears. He stopped just outside the door and placed his hand over his abdomen, squeezing tightly, bending slightly, trying to alleviate the dull aching sensation and the coming nausea. The sick feeling was not for him, but for her.

He could easily put up with the off-color remarks, snickers, and whispers of small-town men and women who would soon receive this bit of big-time gossip, but what about her? It would destroy this beautifully spiritual woman he had learned to love so deeply. A groan escaped from deep within him. "What am I going to do?" he moaned.

Over the next few hours, Joseph completed a massive, strong table that he had begun three days earlier for the town butcher and the two chairs he had promised a widow down the street. Usually this work would take the slow-but-sure carpenter three days to complete. But as Joseph's mind raced for a solution to his dilemma, so did his masterful and strong hands. As he thought about Mary's radiant smile and sweet spirit, his first inclination was to just go ahead and marry her. However, the chance of Mary's pregnancy being discovered and the ominous threat of her being stoned for adultery quickly cleared that idea from his mind. At midnight, as he was sweeping up the last bit of shavings and sawdust, he suddenly stopped and said aloud, "That's it; that's what I'll do. I'll dismiss her quietly and get her out of town. With all the divorces going on today, her abrupt departure will feed a short-lived firestorm of gossip, and then it will be over and she will be safe. She can move to a new town where no one will know we hadn't yet married, and she can get on with her life. Being known as a divorcée is better than being stoned for adultery. That's it; that's it."

Relieved to finally have a plan, Joseph sat down, picked up a wineskin, and drank deeply from it. Suddenly the fatigue from work and worry set in, and he decided to lay his head down on a bench and rest before tackling a couple of projects he was finishing for his own house. Sleep came quickly.

In the depths of sleep, Joseph suddenly sensed a cool breeze brushing his cheek, and the refreshing fragrance of the ocean mingled with the sweetness of lilacs filled his nostrils. But what he was most aware of was the song. It was the most beautiful song he had ever heard, and the soothing words filled his soul with assurance and security. Feeling an arm around him, he turned in his dream and found himself looking directly into the broad smile of an angel. Joseph immediately fell to his knees. Without hesitation the angel knelt in front of him. Joseph was filled with fright at the massive arms and broad, flowing wings, but the angel placed his hands on Joseph's shoulders and spoke in a tone that

Chapter 2

erased all of Joseph's fears. "Joseph, son of David, do not be afraid to take Mary home as your wife. What is conceived in her is from the Holy Spirit. She will give birth to a son, and you are to give Him the name Jesus, because He will save His people from their sins."

At this, the angel stood, spread his enormous wings, and flew from Joseph's presence. As soon as the angel was out of sight, Joseph woke from his dream. The first rays of light had just entered the room and were slowly making their way toward the young carpenter. He was amazingly alert—almost as though he had never been asleep—and he could still sense the fragrance of lilacs on the breeze.

He slowly arose from his seat, went to the window that faced the rising sun, and knelt with his hands lifted high. Tears streamed from his eyes, flowing down his cheeks and into his dark beard as he spoke in a whisper: "I worship You, O Lord; I worship You. I pledge my strength, my soul, and my life to You. Your praise will be on my lips and in my heart forever, for You have blessed this lowly servant with the riches of heaven." He began to rise, then hesitated and sank once more to his knees, adding with emphasis, "Thank You for my Mary, Lord. I will love her and the child You have placed within her with a fiercely protective love. The kind of love You have for me."

Joseph's Dilemma

As he ended his prayer, he stood and bounded from his shop, singing the song he had heard in his dream. He ran quickly to Mary's house, where he found her sweeping her doorway. Her eyes were swollen and red from a night of weeping for the man she loved. He took the broom from her hands and softly said, "Mary, a heavenly messenger gave me the most welcomed news of my life last night. And I have pledged to God that I will love you and the child He has given us, just as He has loved me."

Mary's expression turned from sadness to astonishment when Joseph said "us." Her knees buckled as she felt released from the fear of facing the future without Joseph, and she softly repeated his message: "You said 'us.'" With the warmest smile she had ever seen on Joseph's face, he replied slowly and strongly, "Yes, us."

Joseph lifted Mary to her feet, and as they made their way down the busy street, he told her all about the angel and taught her his newly learned heavenly tune while he brushed the night's sawdust and wood shavings from his beard and off of his clothes.

Joseph's Dilemma

Matthew 1:18–24

This is how the birth of Jesus Christ came about: His mother Mary was pledged to be married to Joseph, but before they came together, she was found to be with child through the Holy Spirit. Because Joseph her husband was a righteous man and did not want to expose her to public disgrace, he had in mind to divorce her quietly.

But after he had considered this, an angel of the Lord appeared to him in a dream and said, "Joseph son of David, do not be afraid to take Mary home as your wife, because what is conceived in her is from the Holy Spirit. She will give birth to a son, and you are to give him the name Jesus, because he will save his people from their sins."

All this took place to fulfill what the Lord had said through the prophet: "The virgin will be with child and will give birth to a son, and they will call him Immanuel"— which means, "God with us."

When Joseph woke up, he did what the angel of the Lord had commanded him and took Mary home as his wife.

As Joseph Was A-Walking

As Joseph was a-walking
He heard Angels sing,
"This night shall be born
Our Heavenly King.

"He neither shall be born
In house nor in hall,
Nor in the place of paradise,
But in an ox-stall.

"He shall not be clothed
In purple nor pall;
But all in fair linen,
As wear babies all.

"He shall not be rocked
In silver nor gold,
But in a wooden cradle
That rocks on the mould.

"He neither shall be christened
In milk nor in wine,
But in pure spring-well water
Fresh spring from Bethine."

Mary took her baby,
She dressed Him so sweet,
She laid Him in a manger,
All there for to sleep.

As she stood over Him
She heard Angels sing,
"Oh, bless our dear Saviour
Our Heavenly King!"

—Anonymous

Christmas Reflections

Have you ever noticed that Christmas comes at just the right time? Think about it. It comes during the very last week of the very last month of the year. Over the preceding months, struggles have been encountered, pain has been endured, joys and sorrows have been shared.

Then, just as you are about to do it all again in a new year, comes this day of celebration with its magnificent story of heavenly visitation and intervention. And at the heart of the story is a promise that brings strength when you feel weak, warmth when you feel alone, and hope when days are dark. This promise was delivered from the tongues of angels to the fearful hearts of Mary, Joseph, and the shepherds. And if you listen carefully, you will hear it in the soft cries of an infant lying in a manger. The promise is for you too. Are you ready? Here it is: Do not fear; God is here. Say it to yourself until its truth echoes into the coming year.

Have you learned some devastating news that has

caused you to despair? Do not fear; God is here. Do you face some uncertainties in the near future? Do not fear; God is here. He knows your heartaches, headaches, pains, and pressures. They all came to rest in His hands, feet, and side. He came to heal the leper, raise the paralytic, and open the blind eyes of the beggar. There is no storm His presence cannot calm.

Prepare yourself for the valleys and peaks of the next year by standing on the summit of this holiday season and breathing in the fragrance of God's presence and promises. Write down your past troubles and your fears about the future and present them to God in prayer. Place them in a box, wrap them up, and write on the tag: Do not fear; God is here. Search through the Scriptures, find all of the "do not be afraid" passages, and read one each day throughout the month of December. You should never face tomorrow until you are filled with God's promise for today.

Yes, Christmas comes at just the right time every year, leading us into the next year with the firm assurance that whatever we encounter, we can safely say: Do not fear; God is here.

Faith is deliberate CONFIDENCE *in the* character *of God* *whose ways* *you cannot* UNDERSTAND *at the time.*

—Oswald Chambers

3

Mary's *Song*

"Why am I so favored, that the mother of my Lord should come to me? As soon as the sound of your greeting reached my ears, the baby in my womb leaped for joy."

ARY AROSE WITH THE RICH smell of spring rain filling her small room. She went to her window and opened her eyes wide as if to allow a full measure of morning light into her waking body. She had slept in complete peace and security after her joyful meeting with Joseph, and today was a day she looked forward to with eager anticipation. She would hurry to see her cousin Elizabeth and tell her all the amazing and wonderful events that had happened and that were filling her heart.

Mary backed away from the window and knelt so that the sun, showing through the clearing sky, shone directly on her face. "My God, O holy God, You are my strength, my hope, and my courage. You fill the morning with Your sweet breath as the fragrance of heaven wakes the earth, and You have filled me with Your child. So much of what You have given me remains a mystery, but as this child grows, so does my love for You. Help me as I share this mystery with Elizabeth, and help her understand not only what You have done for me, but also what You have done for her, as the angel told me." Although Mary didn't really know how God could help her relay to Elizabeth this astonishing news, she knew He would.

As she stood, she looked down at her midsection and ran her hand over her abdomen. Even though the young

Chapter 3

Mary still felt some apprehension about the miracle birth, she found herself wishing she were showing more. She spoke lovingly, sweetly, to the invisible, heaven-sent child who was taking form inside her. "What will You look like, little one? Will You be different from other children?" She let out a small laugh as she said, "Of course You will; You will be the most beautiful child ever born. People will stop me and say, 'What a beautiful child you have—a real gift of God.'" Then she bent her head toward her belly and whispered—as if she were sharing a secret with her infant—"They won't know how right they are."

Mary continued to speak affectionately to the divine life within her as she dressed quickly and set out for the hill country of Judah, where Elizabeth and Zechariah lived.

As she crossed over the last hill before entering the small town that was the home of her beloved relatives, she paused. Mary especially cherished this country at sunset. A bright orange glow radiated from the surrounding hills as they reflected the setting sun's last barrage of light before giving way to darkness. She took this opportunity to carefully rehearse the words she had chosen to say to Elizabeth in explaining the angel's visit and the miracle child she was carrying. She softly prayed, "Please help her understand, my God." She couldn't have known she would never get the chance to recite the lines she had so diligently practiced.

Elizabeth brushed an errant strand of thick, graying hair back into its place as she stood over the remnants of the meal she and her husband had shared. It had been a silent supper for Zechariah, as had all the meals since the angel had silenced his tongue for doubting God's power to give him a child. However, Elizabeth filled these moments with her excited, one-sided conversations about the baby's coming and the plans she had. Zechariah would just smile and nod at his precious Elizabeth's joy. Throughout her barren years, Zechariah had ached over the whispered insults of neighbors and Elizabeth's self-inflicted shame. Now her joy at the coming event took much of the sting out of his punishment.

As Elizabeth prepared to stack the dishes, she heard Mary enter the door and call out her name. As soon as she heard Mary's voice, something extraordinary happened that surprised them both. The baby within Elizabeth became so active she could hardly remain on her feet. She held on to her chair and bent at the waist until the infant calmed. She was then filled with the Holy Spirit, and in a loud voice, she exclaimed: "Blessed are you among women, and blessed is the child you will bear! But why am I so favored, that the mother of my Lord should come to me? As soon as the sound of your greeting reached my ears, the baby in my womb leaped for joy."

Mary's eyes opened wide in surprise even as they flooded with tears, and her hand rushed to cover her mouth, which was open in utter amazement. God had delivered the message of her pregnancy for her. She hadn't had to utter a word. In shock, she whispered to herself, "You know; you know."

Elizabeth moved to Mary, pulled her close, and like a calming mother, laid Mary's head on her shoulder, and swayed from side to side. She then delivered the unexpected message from God to His beloved Mary. Although it came in the form of Elizabeth's soft voice, Mary knew that it originated in heaven and that it held a deliberate assurance. It was said slowly and deliberately so it would not need to be repeated: "Blessed is she who has believed that what the Lord has said to her will be accomplished!"

> As soon as those words reached Mary's heart, she nearly collapsed in awe as she fully understood how much God loved her.

As soon as those words reached Mary's heart, she nearly collapsed in awe as she fully understood how much God loved her. It seemed that all the remaining fear and apprehension at the coming events had been washed away by this one soothing sentence, and she was keenly aware of the impact the life within her would have on the coming generations. She lowered her head, and as Elizabeth brushed her hand over her smooth, dark hair, Mary continued her day as she had begun it: "My soul glorifies the Lord, and my spirit rejoices in God my Savior, for He has been mindful of the humble state of His servant. From now on all generations will call me blessed, for the Mighty One has done great things for me—holy is His name. His mercy extends to those who fear Him, from generation to generation. He has performed mighty deeds with His arm; He has scattered those who are proud in their inmost thoughts. He has brought down rulers from their thrones but has lifted up the humble. He has filled the hungry with good things but has sent the rich away empty. He has helped His servant Israel, remembering to be merciful to Abraham and his descendants forever, even as He said to our fathers."

When Mary finished her prayer, she and Elizabeth rose together. They walked slowly to the table, arm in arm, as Mary excitedly told Elizabeth all that had happened and all that was filling her heart. Mary stayed with Elizabeth for about three months and then returned home. She felt no more fear from that day forward, and all of heaven was pleased.

Mary's Song

Luke 1:39–56

At that time Mary got ready and hurried to a town in the hill country of Judea, where she entered Zechariah's home and greeted Elizabeth. When Elizabeth heard Mary's greeting, the baby leaped in her womb, and Elizabeth was filled with the Holy Spirit. In a loud voice she exclaimed: "Blessed are you among women, and blessed is the child you will bear! But why am I so favored, that the mother of my Lord should come to me? As soon as the sound of your greeting reached my ears, the baby in my womb leaped for joy. Blessed is she who has believed that what the Lord has said to her will be accomplished!"

And Mary said: "My soul glorifies the Lord and my

spirit rejoices in God my Savior, for he has been mindful of the humble state of his servant. From now on all generations will call me blessed, for the Mighty One has done great things for me—holy is his name.

His mercy extends to those who fear him, from generation to generation.

He has performed mighty deeds with his arm; he has scattered those who are proud in their inmost thoughts.

He has brought down rulers from their thrones but has lifted up the humble.

He has filled the hungry with good things but has sent the rich away empty.

He has helped his servant Israel, remembering to be merciful to Abraham and his descendants forever, even as he said to our fathers."

Mary stayed with Elizabeth for about three months and then returned home.

O Little Town of Bethlehem

O holy Child of Bethlehem!
Descend to us, we pray;
Cast out our sin, and enter in,
Be born in us today.

—Phillips Brooks

Christmas Reflections

It happens every Christmas season. You know what I mean. You say to yourself, "I'm going to enjoy the holidays this year and not get caught up in the rat race." But before you know it, you've stepped on the accelerator of life, and the pedal stays on the floor right through Christmas morning. Your thoughts are filled with what presents you should buy for him, for her, that aunt, this parent, that child, this friend, your boss. You spend endless hours shopping, sorting, wrapping, cleaning, and cooking.

Then you ask yourself, "Where did the magic of Christmas go? When did I lose that childlike wonder and whimsical expectation that should accompany the holidays?" Your growing list of responsibilities had tightened your schedule and tempered your imagination. Endless waves of worry had eroded the hope in your heart. In other words, you grew up, gained speed, and gave in to what the world calls the holiday rush. So how do you rediscover Christmas with a childlike passion and an expectant heart? What can you do to uncover the beauty and innocence of the incarnation?

You can renew your belief in what God did two thousand years ago. You can remember that the reason for the season is not pursuing presents or displaying dazzling decorations or even participating in elaborate parties. The purpose for celebrating this wonderful season lies in a divine birth with a heavenly cause. Majesty came to a manger. The creator of the universe was cradled in the hands of a carpenter. The Son of the Most High was sustained by a mother's milk. Why? Because He wanted to bring you peace.

So slow down your pace and ponder the enormous love God has for you. Spend less money and more time with those you love. Read the Christmas story and share with loved ones what it means to you. Remember what was said of a virgin girl in need of assurance: "Blessed is she who has believed." And so are you.

WHEREVER WE ARE,
we are the

light

OF GOD'S

goodness.

—Mother Teresa

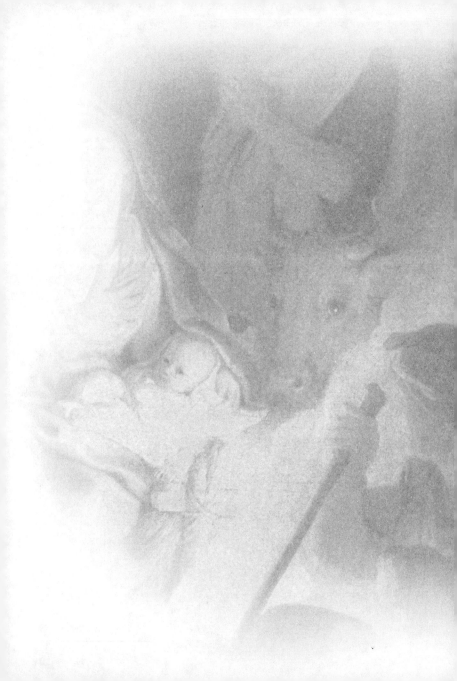

4

The Journey to Bethlehem

Little did the
innkeeper know
that he would be
linked to the Christ
forever in heaven and
earth. For that was
the way God had
planned it all along.

JOSEPH KNEW THAT Mary's plans for the arrival of her baby had not included this hot, dusty, three-day journey to Bethlehem. When Caesar Augustus had issued the decree that every man must go to his hometown to be counted in a census, Joseph had quickly, but skillfully, built a special seat for Mary in his carpentry wagon. Suspended by rope, the seat would absorb some of the shock of the rough terrain they would cover on the way to his hometown.

Mary had wanted badly to have the baby in Nazareth, in familiar surroundings, but with every mile of the bumpy road, the rumblings of the child served as warning that she might not make it back to her beloved town for the blessed event.

Joseph was well aware of Mary's discomfort, and though she never complained, he sensed that the time was upon them. He attempted to take her mind off the baby by filling the hours with tales of his childhood in Bethlehem. Mary laughed at his antics, and for a short time, they relieved her concern. But there weren't enough stories to last the many miles ahead. When Joseph ran out of sagas to distract her, he noticed that Mary had totally immersed herself in prayer.

In the heat of the afternoon of the third day, Joseph thought it would be wise to stop before the last push into

Bethlehem. He built a covering with a cloth attached to stilts, which he stuck deep in the dirt so they could rest in the cool of some shade. He knelt beside Mary and watched her gently massage her midsection, then he looked into her beautiful, deep eyes. "We didn't plan for this, did we?"

Mary smiled shyly, running her soft fingers across Joseph's weathered brow. "No," she replied gently. "And you didn't plan to marry a pregnant virgin, and I didn't plan to have a child planted in me by the hand of God." She gazed at the bright blue sky as she continued: "But Joseph, with every mile we travel, I get a stronger and stronger sense that this is exactly what He has planned, and I trust Him completely."

Dusk was approaching when the young couple reached the Bethlehem city limits, and Mary couldn't help but admire the most beautiful sunset she had ever witnessed. At the thin line that separated earth and sky, a rainbow of yellows and reds hung above the earth, announcing the coming night. There were no clouds or wind; the heavens were calm and peaceful. The streets, however, were packed with weary travelers, shopkeepers, and street vendors, all jostling to find a place to stay or provide some needed service. After Joseph visited with several people who had already found shelter for the night, he knew that the only place to go was the town inn. Joseph arrived just as the innkeeper was renting the last room.

As the young couple approached, the innkeeper reached out his hand, grasped Joseph's hand enthusiastically, and looked beyond him at the very pregnant and obviously uncomfortable Mary. The man's name was Daniel—after the prophet— and the name represented the man's faith accurately. His hair was black with a few strands of gray, he was a bit heavyset, and his breathing was labored as he spoke. Under thick eyelids, his bright, joyful eyes bespoke of his kind heart and warm spirit. His expression

> "With every mile we travel, I get a stronger and stronger sense that this is exactly what He has planned."

reflected sincere concern as Joseph explained their dilemma. "I'm sorry, children," he said, "but I have nowhere for you to stay. I have even given up my own room for this throng of people; otherwise, I would gladly give it to you."

Seeing the dejection painted on Joseph's face, Daniel walked around the corner and then came back to them. "Listen, I know it probably isn't what you'd planned, but I have a stable in the back, and you can stay there free of charge."

Chapter 4

Joseph searched Mary's face and found a strangely intuitive smile. "That will be fine, I guess," Joseph replied.

As Daniel led them to the stable, he stopped and said, "You know, I can hardly believe I offered you this place. I hadn't planned on anyone staying here tonight—especially someone who is going to have a baby—but oddly enough, it feels that this is the way it's supposed to be." The innkeeper stepped into the stable and began sweeping up a great mound of hay with his legs. Mary was touched as she noticed Daniel's breathing growing heavier from what for him was an enormous effort. When he had done all he could to prepare her bed, he turned to Mary and said, "I hope you sleep well, dear child. Do not hesitate to call on me for anything you need. May God bless you."

> "My God, this is just a stable; but once Your Son enters, it will be the most beautiful place on earth."

As Joseph and Daniel stood outside and talked for a minute more, Mary knelt in the straw where she would soon have her child and prayed. "My God, I know you have brought me here to have Your child. Now, this is just a stable; but once Your Son enters, it will be the most beautiful place on earth—for that is how You've planned it. May I accomplish Your will." With that, Mary prepared herself and a place in the straw for the coming of Jesus.

As the kind Daniel walked away, he repeated again and again, "If you need anything, children, don't hesitate to ask. I am not far away." He was true to his word and true in his heart to the young couple. Little did he know that he would be linked to the Christ forever in heaven and earth. For that was the way God had planned it all along.

The *Journey* to Bethlehem

Luke 2:1–7

In those days Caesar Augustus issued a decree that a census should be taken of the entire Roman world.... And everyone went to his own town to register.

So Joseph also went up from the town of Nazareth in Galilee to Judea, to Bethlehem the town of David, because he belonged to the house and line of David. He went there to register with Mary, who was pledged to be married to him and was expecting a child. While they were there, the time came for the baby to be born, and she gave birth to her firstborn, a son. She wrapped him in cloths and placed him in a manger, because there was no room for them in the inn.

$\mathcal{W}$ere earth a thousand times as fair,

Beset with gold and jewels rare,

She yet were far too poor to be

A narrow cradle, Lord, for Thee.

—Martin Luther

Christmas Reflections

There is one question that you will both ask and answer a multitude of times during the holidays. You'll hear it from friends, family, coworkers, and neighbors, and everyone who asks will genuinely want to know the answer to this: "What are your plans for the holidays?" You probably will be able to answer with amazing detail, and those you ask will be able to do the same—even if Christmas is still a month away. There seems to be no other time when we plan our activities so carefully, prepare for events so competently, or chart our lives so completely. Go ahead, mark your calendar, map out your course, make a detailed list, prepare for the parties, plan out the menus, and send out the invitations. But this year, add a note on your calendar that says, "Leave room for God's plans."

The most rewarding experiences of our lives can come during the holidays, when we free our schedules and open our eyes to the unexpected surprises of a loving God. You might be on the way to the grocery store when you meet a hungry soul or on your way to visit a neighbor when you run into someone with a lonely heart. You may go to a party and encounter a stranger who desperately needs a word of encouragement. These divine appointments cannot be planned or charted; they just happen. And you don't want to miss a single one, because these unplanned encounters may just change history.

God planned it that way.

The hinge
of history
IS ON THE DOOR
of a Bethlehem
STABLE.
—Ralph W. Sockman

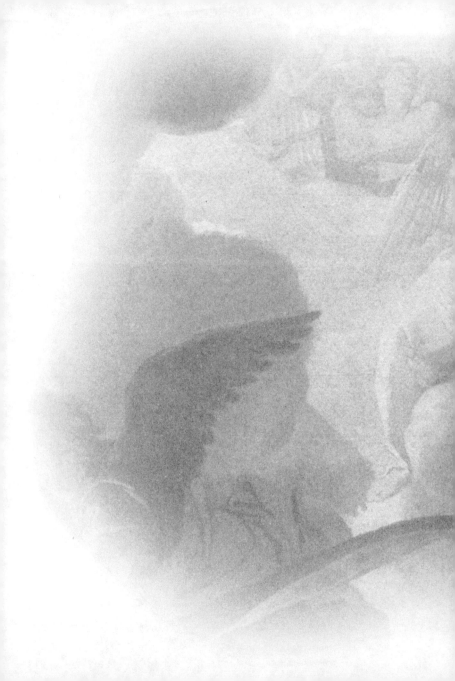

5

The Birth

Joseph didn't know
exactly how, but he
was keenly aware that
not only his life but
the lives of all people
everywhere were about
to change.

I T WAS ALMOST MIDNIGHT when Joseph stepped from the stable for a moment's rest as Mary's labor temporarily subsided. He rubbed his eyes with the palms of his hands and then ran his hands down the length of his beard. He vigorously pounded his chest and arms until he felt fully alert. The silence of the surrounding night was overwhelming. He looked up and down the barren streets and listened to the stillness.

Just a few hours before, people had crowded the streets with laughter, friendly conversation, tearful reunions, and political dialogue. He had thought to himself, then, that no one in these city streets—or for that matter, in the whole world—knew what wonderful miracle would soon take place inside this stable. Not just a miracle of new life, but also the miracle of a visitor from heaven who would somehow impact their world for eternity. Joseph didn't know exactly how, but he was keenly aware that not only his life but the lives of all people everywhere were about to change.

At one point in the evening—when the full weight of this realization landed in his heart—he had nearly jumped up and run into the streets to tell anyone who would listen. But the cold water of logic doused his enthusiasm when he realized he didn't know what he would say. How could he explain that God had chosen Mary, a virgin, and himself, a poor carpenter, to bring His own special child into the world? Or that the blessed event was about to happen in a hay-filled, animal-housing stable? *Sure thing, Joseph,* he thought to himself with a laugh. *They would surely believe that, wouldn't they?*

Now, as he stood alone in the night, Joseph stretched out his arms as wide as they would reach, took a deep breath, and looked up at the diamond-filled sky. The moonless night enhanced the glow of the stars so that they formed a blanket of brilliant light. He silently asked himself when he had last been so stunned by the sheer beauty of an Israel night.

The wonder of it all triggered something in the young carpenter. The joy of a future shared with his beloved Mary and this soon-to-be-born child, whom he would name Jesus, swept over him like a refreshing rain. He began to dance under the night sky and sang out in a loud voice, "What a blessed man you are, Joseph; what a blessed man you are." He stopped, arched his back, and spoke to the attentive stars. "Stars, shimmer like you have never shimmered before, because I will soon introduce you to my son, Jesus, and I want you to look your very best."

He turned to the quiet, empty streets of the city

and cried out with pride and joy. "Bethlehem, my beloved Bethlehem, you have been the home of King David and his mighty men. You have seen the greatest rulers of the world. But you have never seen anything like you will see tonight. Within your bosom is one who will make you worth more than if your buildings were covered in gold and your streets were lined with silver." As he heard Mary groan in the pains of childbirth, Joseph whispered, "And there is a woman in our midst of whom neither you nor I are worthy." Suddenly Mary's strained voice called out for him, and he went in to help deliver the coming child.

How could he explain that God had chosen Mary, a virgin, and himself, a poor carpenter, to bring His own special child into the world?

After cutting the umbilical cord with his knife, Joseph carefully picked up the baby and cradled Him in his arms. He ever so tenderly touched the soft skin of the infant, fearing that his rough hands might harm this delicate treasure. Mary's face filled with pride as she watched her husband cuddle God's child. When Jesus began to whimper, Mary took Him into her arms, wrapped Him in strips of cloth, and laid Him down in the manger. Mary and

Joseph looked into each other's eyes and smiled as they brushed the tears from their cheeks. "Jesus, meet Joseph," Mary said to her child. "Joseph, meet Jesus."

Joseph responded playfully, "Where have You been, little Jesus? We've been waiting for You for so long." His words trailed off as he repeated soberly, again and again, "for so long…"

Joseph scooped the child up into his arms. "Mary, I have to introduce Jesus to someone; I'll be right back."

> He turned Jesus toward the city and said, "Jesus, meet Bethlehem. You have brought this old city great honor tonight."

Joseph walked with deliberation and pride into the starry night. He looked up at the heavens and said, "Jesus, meet all the stars of heaven. They are shimmering just for You. I told them You were coming, and they put on their very best lights—just for You." Then he turned Jesus toward the city and said, "Jesus, meet Bethlehem. You have brought this old city great honor tonight. It is very proud that You are here." He then brushed his lips against Jesus' forehead and said softly, "But most of all, You have honored me tonight, and I am very proud that You're here."

Isaiah 9:6

For to us a child is born, to us a son is given,
and the government will be on his shoulders.
And he will be called Wonderful Counselor,
Mighty God, Everlasting Father, Prince of Peace.

Matthew 2:16

When Herod realized that he had been out-witted by the Magi, he was furious, and he gave orders to kill all the boys in Bethlehem and its vicinity who were two years old and under, in accordance with the time he had learned from the Magi.

A little child,
a shining star,
A stable, rude,
the door ajar.
Yet in that place
so crude, forlorn,
The Hope of all the
world was born.

—*Anonymous*

Christmas Reflections

If you were asked to make a comprehensive list of words associated with Christmas, you probably would find the task quite simple. Words such as *love, joy, peace, goodwill, giving, fun, family,* and *friendship* would pour from your lips with ease.

However, there is another word, perhaps less likely to make your list, that really should stand above all others. It is a word that forces us to examine the real meaning of Christmas, much the way a jeweler peers into the depths of a precious stone to assess its value. For just as the sparkle of a precious gem begins within its core, every other glowing term used to describe heaven's visit to our world begins at the core of what God did for us. The word is *honored.* Yes, *honored.* On that glorious day two thousand years ago, God honored you and me with His presence.

In light of the poverty, pain, and peril He knew He would face in our world, He could have chosen to stay home. Instead, He tore the curtains that separated the divine from the dishonored, blasted through the walls that divided perfection from the perverse, and broke down the doors that isolated royalty from the rabble. And because it might be difficult for us to identify with Him if He came to a palace or a castle, He honored our simplicity by being born in a stable, through the womb of a young woman.

Take out your magnifying glass and look back at the scene of His birth. Smell the musty odors of the stable; listen to the heavy breathing of a virgin who has just given birth to the Savior. View the face of a rough-handed carpenter who cradled our eternal destiny in His hands.

But above all, don't miss the infant. See the small body that traveled all the way from heaven. Hear Him cry for His mother's milk. Feel the soft flesh of a newborn who came to save the world. And never, ever forget that you are the reason He came.

During the holidays we honor Him for who He is. But He came and honored us with His presence because He knew what we could become.

WHEN IT

etern

fo

PURPOSE,

go to the

WHEN IT COMES TO *eternity,* *forgiveness,* PURPOSE, AND TRUTH; *go to the manger.* Kneel with the shepherds. *And worship* THE GOD *who dared to do* WHAT MAN DARED NOT *dream.*

—Max Lucado

6

God's Message for the Shepherds

Not only were they bound together by their ostracism, but they also shared a profound awareness of their responsibility.

ETH'S CHEST SWELLED as he inhaled deeply, enjoying the sweet, mixed fragrance of fresh vegetation and salty sea that had drifted to Bethlehem on a gentle southwest wind. It was a welcome scent after a grueling day of tending dust-raising, grass-eating, musty-smelling sheep.

At this time of night, every night, while the herds slept, five of the shepherds from the surrounding fields came together and conversed about family, shepherding, money, politics, and anything else that came to mind. All five of them—Seth, Eli, Jonathan, Asa, and Matthan—were third-generation shepherds. Although most of the citizenry of Israel looked down on their occupation because it was considered filthy and alienating work, those who lived in cities were totally reliant on shepherds to supply the sacrifices they offered to God. These five men were keenly aware of the disdain the locals felt for them, and their shared estrangement created and sustained a loyal bond of kinship between them. Not only were they bound together by their ostracism, but they also shared a profound awareness of their responsibility to supply the sacrificial lambs for Israel's worship to Almighty God.

Seth lifted a new wineskin and drank deeply from it and then passed it to his companions. Each took his turn and savored the wonderful flavor as the wine washed away the day's dust that had accumulated in their throats. Jonathan, the youngest of the group, with dark hair and skin and bright eyes, spoke first: "Have any of you noticed the silence in the air tonight? Even the sheep are still. I haven't heard a sound from any of them all evening." His eyes darted back and forth over the herd as he looked and listened for movement.

Seth, the oldest in both age and appearance, spoke in a hushed tone. "The silence feels almost reverent, as though the world were waiting for something to happen." Eli, Asa, and Matthan nodded and mumbled their agreement as they ran their fingers through their chest-length beards.

Matthan felt a shiver run through him and attempted to change the subject. "Have any of you heard the news that is spreading all over Judea about the priest Zechariah?" The others exchanged puzzled expressions and shook their heads.

"What news, brother?" Eli asked.

"Well, no one can explain it, but his wife, Elizabeth, was barren."

"What's so interesting about that?" Seth chided.

"Let me finish the story, Seth," Matthan said, as he playfully pushed Seth off the stone where he sat. Matthan started again. "Listen, his wife was barren until he went into the temple of the Lord. According to him, an angel was standing at the right side of the altar of incense."

Jonathan's eyes were wide open, pleading with Matthan to continue, and he asked, "You mean a real angel from heaven?"

"Yes—a real angel," answered Matthan confidently.

"He had to be making that up," Eli scoffed.

"Well, listen to this," Matthan continued. "The angel told him that his wife would have the son they had been praying for and that this child would bring people back to God and prepare them for the coming of the Lord. When Zechariah demonstrated his doubt that such a thing could actually happen, the angel silenced his tongue. When the priest walked out of the temple, he couldn't make a sound."

"What happened next?" Jonathan begged.

"Well, after he went home, sure enough, his wife became pregnant, and she had a son just three months ago. And it wasn't until Zechariah named him John, like the angel had told him to do, that he could finally speak again."

> "The silence feels almost reverent, as though the world were waiting for something to happen."

Chapter 6

Eli said aloud what the others were thinking. "What could all this mean?"

But Seth mocked them cynically. "Angels from heaven—I don't believe it!"

Just as Seth was closing his mouth, an angel of the Lord appeared out of nowhere, and the glory of the Lord shone all around them. The five frightened shepherds jumped up and ran toward the hills. But as he was running, Seth stumbled and fell to the ground; he lay frozen in fear. Then the angel picked Seth up and spoke to them all with a calming voice, beckoning them to return. "Do not be afraid. I bring you good news of great joy that will be for all the people."

A stunned Jonathan leaned over to Eli and in a trembling voice said, "Do you think he will silence our tongues too?"

Eli replied nervously, "Brother, I just hope to get out of this with my life—I don't care about my tongue!"

As the angel smiled and continued in a soothing voice, the shepherds began to calm. "Today, in the town of David, a Savior has been born to you; He is Christ the

> Suddenly the heavens were filled with angels, and they were praising God with a song.

Lord. This will be a sign to you: You will find a baby wrapped in cloths and lying in a manger."

Suddenly the heavens were filled with angels, and they were praising God with a song. The shepherds—now assured they were in no danger and overjoyed by the news—joined in the song and began dancing under the host of angels. Then, as the song echoed through the night, the angels left them.

With the fields still once again, all that could be heard was the panting of the shepherds. They looked at each other, then embraced and danced delightedly. "What do we do now?" they asked in unison.

"Let's go to Bethlehem and see this thing that has happened, which the Lord has told us about," said Seth. So they hurried off and found Mary and Joseph and the baby, who was lying in the manger. They timidly approached the couple and the sleeping baby. But their shyness evaporated at Mary and Joseph's radiant faces, and they excitedly relayed what had happened and why they had come.

Asa spoke up after their story had been told. "I know this must sound unbelievable to the two of you."

But Joseph and Mary just looked at each other and smiled. "Strangely enough," Joseph said, "it isn't hard to believe at all."

Chapter 6

Haltingly, Seth asked Mary, "Could I touch the head of my Lord?"

Without saying a word, Mary lifted the cover, exposing the head of the child. One by one, each shepherd came forward, placed a hand on Jesus' head, and blessed Him. Tears ran down weathered cheeks that had not felt the wet warmth for years.

When they had seen Jesus, they spread the word concerning what had been told to them about this child, and all who heard it were amazed at what the shepherds said. The five men returned to their fields, glorifying and praising God for all the things they had heard and seen, which were just as they had been told.

> After that sacred night, the small group continued to meet in the fields while their sheep slept.

After that sacred night, the small group continued to meet in the fields while their sheep slept. They still spoke of family and shepherding, but mostly they spoke about the goodness of the God they served. He had sent a special message to lowly shepherds about a royal birth. They, of all people, had been among the first to hear the announcement, delivered by angels. They had heard the angelic host sing a heavenly song of hope. They—lowly shepherds—had been among the first to see the Savior, who himself would be both shepherd and sheep for the world.

No one in Bethlehem ever looked down on shepherding again.

God's Message for the Shepherds

Luke 2:8–20

And there were shepherds living out in the fields nearby, keeping watch over their flocks at night. An angel of the Lord appeared to them, and the glory of the Lord shone around them, and they were terrified. But the angel said to them, "Do not be afraid. I bring you good news of great joy that will be for all the people. Today in the town of David a Savior has been born to you; he is Christ the Lord. This will be a sign to you: You will find a baby wrapped in cloths and lying in a manger."

Suddenly a great company of the heavenly host appeared with the angel, praising God and saying, "Glory to God in the highest, and on earth peace to men on whom his favor rests."

When the angels had left them and gone into heaven, the shepherds said to one another, "Let's go to Bethlehem and see this thing that has happened, which the Lord has told us about."

So they hurried off and found Mary and Joseph, and the baby, who was lying in the manger. When they had seen him, they spread the word concerning what had been told them about this child, and all who heard it were amazed at what the shepherds said to them. But Mary treasured up all these things and pondered them in her heart. The shepherds returned, glorifying and praising God for all the things they had heard and seen, which were just as they had been told.

A Christmas Carol

The shepherds went their
  hasty way,
And found the lowly
  stable-shed
Where the virgin-mother lay:
And now they checked their
  eager tread,
For to the babe, that at her
  bosom clung,
A mother's song the
  virgin-mother sung.

They told her how a glorious
    light,
Streaming from a heavenly
    throng,
Around them shone,
    suspending night;
While sweeter than a
    mother's song,
Blessed angels heralded
    the Saviour's birth,
Glory to God on high! and
    peace on earth.
—Samuel Taylor Coleridge

Christmas Reflections

Here's a question for you. You may be inspired to answer immediately, or you may want to contemplate awhile. Feel free to take as much time as you need. Are you ready?

Have you ever experienced a hug from heaven? Have you ever felt the brush of an angel wing that changed your course, sensed a small voice that sent you on an unplanned mission, or experienced a warm embrace of assurance from an unexpected source? Has a much-needed parcel been received just when it could help the most, or has a divine message arrived that filled your drained heart to overflowing with the love of God?

If so, you've most certainly experienced a hug from heaven. And what exactly do these experiences mean? The same thing that God has been trying to tell us since He sent a bear hug from heaven in the form of an infant lying in a manger, surrounded by a proud mom and dad and some very surprised shepherds. Hugs from heaven remind you that you are not alone and that God knows what you need.

What do you do with these hugs from heaven? Let the warmth of their truth live in your heart every day—not just during Christmas—so that when the cold winds of doubt or fear blow on your life (and they will), you can rest assured that there is a strong and caring hand leading you home.

Oh, and don't be surprised if someday, somewhere, you find yourself delivering a hug from heaven to others. They'll probably look just as surprised as the shepherds.

God goes
to those who have time
TO HEAR HIM—
so on a cloudless night
he went to simple
S H E P H E R D S .

—Max Lucado

7

The Angels' Good News

*All of heaven and
earth had looked
forward to this
moment since God
had formed humans
in His image.*

BSOLUTE SILENCE ECHOED in Hallel's ears. No one spoke a word; not a wing fluttered. Even more amazing, the sound of praise and worship that continually echoed through the halls of heaven had ceased. The angel couldn't remember another time like it: Heaven was silent.

Hallel would never have believed there would be a time when he was not leading a heavenly host in a vast assortment of songs and choruses. As the angel of praise, he was ordained to lead heaven in perpetual adulation and ceaseless song, and he carried out his duties joyfully.

The Father had gifted him with a clear, inviting voice that emboldened even the most timid angel to join the worship with wholehearted enthusiasm, and Hallel's face beamed with a constant smile. Even in this uncommon and rather uncomfortable silence, his eyes blazed with anticipation as he thought about the sequence of events that had led to this moment and the miracle that was about to unfold. All of heaven and earth had looked forward to this moment since God had formed humans in His image.

Hallel had been preparing songs of praise for the anticipated event when Gabriel delivered the unsettling message. If the request had not come directly from him, Hallel would have thought it a deception from Lucifer or one of his cohorts. But the excitement in Gabriel's voice and the urgent expression on his face punctuated his plea with authenticity. Gabriel instructed him to leave his perch of praise and fly immediately to the throne room of Almighty God.

Putting Micah, his assistant, in charge of the heavenly chorus, Hallel flew to his meeting with lightning speed. He entered the glorious presence of the Father and covered his face with his wings as he knelt before God, saying, "Glory be to You, Almighty Father. How may I serve You?"

> "How can I keep myself—much less the whole host— quiet in anticipation of Your Son's birth?"

With a voice as beautiful as a comforting wind, the Father spoke. "Hallel, you have served Me well, from the beginning until now. Your brilliant songs of praise have been heard from the depths of the earth to the farthest reaches of the heavens. I know you may be confused by My instructions; however, I am confident you will carry them out as I ask, for you follow Me out of love.

"Very soon, the most wonderful incident of all measured time will take place on earth. Do you know the event of which I speak?"

"Yes, my Lord, I was preparing praises for the birth when You called."

With a broad smile, the Father continued, "Gather your heavenly host and prepare to go where My Son will be born. You are to arrive in Bethlehem on the day of the birth. But when you get there, do not make a sound: no songs, no praise, no speech. You are to be completely silent."

A baffled look swept over Hallel's face. His wings trembled. "No songs of worship?" he asked.

The Father affirmed, "None."

"But, Lord," Hallel boldly protested, "I find it difficult to refrain from breaking into praise just being in Your presence this short time. How can I keep myself—much less the whole host—quiet in anticipation of Your Son's birth?"

The Father's eyes glowed even more brightly than usual. "Hallel, My Son's birth will be a holy occurrence that will never be repeated. The future of the world revolves around the birth of My Son. Hearts will be healed, the dead will be raised, fear will be defeated, and My enemy Satan will no longer be able to steal the joy of My children. Love that has grown stale will be renewed, fullness will replace emptiness, and dreams will become reality. In honor of this sacred moment, the night shall be silent when My Son enters the world. Go in silence and witness this sacred event with the heavenly host nearby. When you hear the first cry from the lips of the infant and see the first quiver of His lips, gather your host and deliver the message of joy that the Savior is born."

Immediately Hallel asked, "Who shall receive this wonderful announcement? Which king or ruler?"

"No dignitary is worthy of this news. Go to the faithful, the poor, and the weak. Go first to the shepherds outside the city of Bethlehem who raise My sacrificial lambs. They shall hear the news first because My Son will be both sheep and shepherd for My people." As the Father spoke, He held out a book. "When you make the announcement, sing this song. Sing it so that it fills heaven and earth and the caverns of hell with the news that victory belongs to the Father and His children."

Hallel looked at the book, smiled with appreciation, and turned, saying, "Your will be done, my Lord and my God."

Hallel immediately gathered his host from their stations across the heavens, and they sang as they made their way to the little town of Bethlehem. Upon the setting of Earth's sun, not another word was uttered by any heavenly being, and the night was silent as never before. As the host waited in the distance, Hallel posted himself inside the stable with Mary and Joseph, awaiting his signal. Unseen, he paced back and forth with Joseph. Hallel winced at the virgin's birth pains, prayed for her relief, and stared in amazement at the first sight of the child's head. As Joseph spoke words of encouragement to Mary, Hallel found himself cheering her on as well. "That's it, Mary. You can do it. Just a little longer."

Then Hallel heard it: the soft cry that was quickly quieted at Mary's breast. Hallel sprang up, flexed his mighty wings, and flew to the waiting host. He wanted to shout for joy to the whole world, but he knew the first words were for the shepherds. He waved to the host to follow him to the nearby fields. There he found the chosen shepherds tending their sheep. He watched for a moment and thought to himself, *These shepherds have no idea that their lives are about to be changed forever.*

Upon the setting of Earth's sun, not another word was uttered by any heavenly being, and the night was silent as never before.

Instantly, he appeared to them in a flash of glory. The shepherds ran backward in fear, but Hallel approached them, glowing with delight. "Do not be afraid. I bring you good news of great joy that will be for all the people." As he spoke, they cautiously moved closer, drawn by his warm smile and inviting voice. "Today, in the town of David, a Savior has been born to you; He is Christ the Lord." The shepherds knelt at the sound of the news. "This will be a sign to you: You will find a baby wrapped in cloths and lying in a manger."

Hallel turned and commanded, "Sing the song the Lord has given us!" The heavenly host appeared and filled the silent night with glorious praise. Hallel joined the throng, and together they sang, "Glory to God in the highest, and on earth, peace to men on whom His favor rests." They sang it again and again, louder with each refrain. The shepherds joined the singing with all their hearts and danced around the flock. As the host retreated, the song hung in the air, a sweet incense of praise.

Hallel followed the shepherds into the town where they found the Savior, just as he had told them. As they knelt in wonder, he knelt invisibly with them, placed his wings around them, and quietly sang again, "Glory to God in the highest, and on earth, peace to men on whom His favor rests."

The *Angels'* Good News

Luke 2:10–16

The angel said to them, "Do not be afraid. I bring you good news of great joy that will be for all the people. Today in the town of David a Savior has been born to you; he is Christ the Lord. This will be a sign to you: You will find a baby wrapped in cloths and lying in a manger."

Suddenly a great company of the heavenly host appeared with the angel, praising God and saying,

"Glory to God in the highest, and on earth peace to men on whom his favor rests."

When the angels had left them and gone into heaven, the shepherds said to one another, "Let's go to Bethlehem and see this thing that has happened, which the Lord has told us about."

So they hurried off and found Mary and Joseph, and the baby, who was lying in the manger.

Angels, from the Realms of Glory

Angels, from the realms of glory,
Wing your flight o'er all the earth;
Ye who sang creation's story,
Now proclaim Messiah's birth:
Come and worship, come and worship,
Worship Christ, the newborn King!

—James Montgomery

Christmas
Reflections

They are only three short words in the middle of the message given by angels about the coming of Christ. Said any other time by any other person, those three words would be an empty promise, never to be realized. However, these are not just hollow words offered by a power-hungry politician seeking reelection. They are not a slogan penned by an organization pleading for money, nor are they the battle cry of a destructive army.

No, these are heavenly words heavy with truth and inhabited with hope: peace on earth.

The one thing earth is in search of, hearts are trying to hold on to, and lives are longing to find is peace. Peace from fear of the future; peace from emotional battle scars; peace from worry about money, career, prestige, prominence, or power; and peace from the frustration of wondering whether anyone really cares.

To all of those concerns, worries, and frustrations comes the message of the season that meets the needs of all life. God sent the Christ so that, on earth, you could find peace.

This is not a peace intended to last only until the decorations of December come down or the bills of January arrive. This is a powerful peace meant to rule in your heart and life every day of every year. Christ is not just a savior for one day during one month of the year; He is the Savior every day of your life. If you want proof, follow your peace away from the manger and into life. See how He brought healing to a paralytic, sight to the blind, hope to a widow who had just lost her son, and forgiveness to everyone as He stretched His arms over two beams of wood and reached across history to embrace you today.

Yes, peace on earth can be found. It starts in a manger, is finished on the cross, and lives in your heart forever—because He's coming again.

IT'S ALL

to he

God has b

THE

we built

IT'S ALL RIGHT
to hope again....
God has broken down
THE PRISON WALLS
we built for ourselves
and has set us
FREE.
A whole new world
of hope
HAS COME INTO BEING.

—Jim McGuiggan

A Christmas Prayer

Loving Father, help us remember the birth of
Jesus, that we may share in the song of the
angels, the gladness of the shepherds, and
the worship of the wise men.

Close the door of hate and open the door of
love all over the world.

Let kindness come with every gift and good
desires with every greeting.

Deliver us from evil by the blessing which Christ brings, and teach us to be merry with clear hearts.

May the Christmas morning make us happy to be Thy children, and the Christmas evening bring us to our beds with grateful thoughts, forgiving and forgiven, for Jesus' sake. Amen!

—*Robert Louis Stevenson*